THE ENCOUNTER WITH WISDOM

THE SECRETS OF HER

"POWERFUL LIFE CHANGING QUOTES"

DR. LARON MATTHEWS PHD

Endorsements for

The Encounter with Wisdom

The Secrets of Her "Powerful Quotes"

by Prophet/Dr. Laron Matthews

Dr. Laron Matthews is a prophetic gift for our times. I'm confident that "The Encounter With Wisdom; The Secret of Her" will not only clarify your faith but strengthen your faith. Whether you're dealing with anger, loneliness, insecurity, or shame, these powerful quotes will serve as helpful resources. Just kick the enemy out of your mind and allow these quotes to strengthen you. These quotes will help with changing the battle of your mind. Congratulations, Dr. Laron Matthews. I am confident that this book will touch lives across the world.

Bishop Gary Wheeler

Changing Your World Church International

Orlando, FL

I am honored to endorse Dr. Laron Matthews's new book, "*The Encounter with Wisdom; The Secrets of Her "Powerful Quotes.*"These powerful quotes will help you find in your heart biblical truths that will help free not only your mind but your life. Thank you, Dr. Laron Matthews, for these powerful quotes that will help us in our daily walk with the Lord.

Evangelist Ellen Allen

Toledo, Oh

The Encounter With Wisdom The Secrets Of Her "Powerful Quotes"

BY PROPHET/DR. LARON MATTHEWS

Congratulations, son, this book has blessed our entire family, and we're so grateful to God to be your parents and dedicating this book to your mother just blesses my heart. We love you son.

Bishop Nathaniel Matthews

The Way of Life Holiness Church

Joilet, IL

Now is the time that we, as Children of the Kingdom of God, come to know a deeper experience and mind of GOD. How so? When GOD said for His children to seek ye first the Kingdom of GOD, it is more than words on a page. What is the key behind us seeking the Kingdom of GOD? It is Wisdom! For this reason, believers need to know all we can concerning such a vast topic. The Bible has declared unto this people in Ephesian 3:3-5, "How that by revelation he made known unto me the mystery; (as I wrote afore in few words, ⁴Whereby, when ye read, ye may understand my knowledge in the mystery of Christ) ⁵Which in other ages was not made known unto the sons of men, as it is now revealed unto his holy apostles and prophets by the Spirit.

All praises to GOD for pressing it upon His servant, Prophet Dr. Laron Matthews, to release insight and knowledge that concerns the subject of Wisdom. As a Kingdom Leader and supporter of Dr. Matthews' Ministry since 2012, I can say that the Secret of Wisdom has been forthcoming and is being presented in this book. I am sure that you will be delighted and comforted by the words that are printed on its pages. Congrats to you, my leader and friend, on your second publication that will awaken Zion dwellers.

Dr. Carlina A. Wilkes

Evangelist, Pastor and Teacher

Chosen Generation Ministries, Inc.

Dr. Laron Matthews has masterfully illustrated a powerful must-read book. This book, 'The Encounter with Wisdom, the Secret of Her,' personifies the wisdom God releases and affords to every person.

God's mind is filled with indescribable brilliance, and He has granted us access to His infinite wisdom and understanding. 'For who has known the mind of the Lord, that He may instruct Him? But we have the mind of Christ.' (1 Corinthians 2:16, NKJV)

As a man of God, leader, overseer, pastor, and mentor, I personally recognize the necessity of God's wisdom. We must pray and seek the face of God daily for His wisdom in order to be effective in every relationship and aspect of life (husband, father, son, friend, leader, etc.).

I thank God for the covenant relationship with Dr. Laron Matthews. The godly wisdom he imparts as a spiritual father, mentor, leader, and friend to a spiritual son such as myself is phenomenal and life-changing. He is a man full of God's wisdom.

I pray that all who read this book will encounter God's wisdom in an extraordinary way and allow the secret of God's eternal riches to fill their lives.

"H.E.R"~ HIS Eternal Riches

Apostle Maurice Simmons

Oversee and Pastor

Restoration and Truth Ministries

Hampton, VA

*This book is dedicated to **Mother Ellen Allen**, for her love, support, encouragement, and strength.*

Thank you for being in my life.

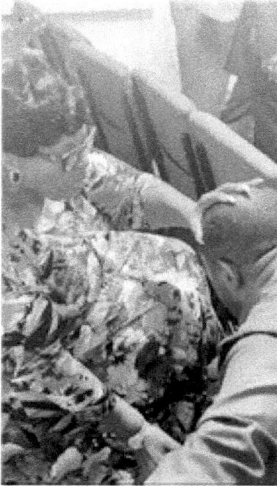

I also would like to dedicate this book, *The Encounter with Wisdom; The Secret of Her* to my phenomenal mother **Susan Matthews** who bore 18 children of which I am the seventh child. Thank you for dedicating your life, career, and years to the nurturing of your children and for the impeccable love you gave to us all. It's through your life that I first encountered the pulse of Wisdom which activated a desire within me to know Her. Thank you, Mother, for the relentless pour of wisdom and love.

For many years, as the 7th child among 18 siblings, my mom has always carried us. This picture symbolizes the wisdom that now allows me to carry her.

In Memory of my sister

Regina Ann Matthews

May this book be a breath of fresh air to all who read it and may you experience the activation pulse of Wisdom.

INTRODUCTION

Life can be very demanding, and oftentimes it presents us with situations that can cause confusion when we don't understand how to navigate the things that stand before us. Of greater importance however, is the fact that with proper tools and guidance we can overcome them. The Bible declares that wisdom is the principal thing and that in all our getting we should get an understanding. Wisdom gives insight, foresight, and illumination which brings understanding and direction. This book was written to provide you with practical tools to help you to navigate through the challenging and hazy periods of life

The quotes in this book were born during some of the most passionate and intimate moments with my Father. I believe this book is not only relevant to your everyday life and its challenges, but it also carries the ability to alter your life, and position you on the right path to peace, freedom, and victory.

My experience in ministry has taught me a lot about the human condition, and the power of love and words to transform lives. I have dealt with people from every walk of life with many different challenges, from childhood traumas, addictions, failures, struggles, failed marriages, Christian backsliding, and the list goes on. It is the observation and interaction with these experiences that led me on a journey with the Holy Spirit to understand and provide the tools and solutions to these woes.

On this journey the secrets of "Her wisdom" were revealed. The Bible declares that all the paths of wisdom are peace. If all the paths of wisdom are peace, then we must apply wisdom in every aspect of our lives.

The power of words infused by the wisdom of God is so important to our lives. I believe that everyone should have a watchword, a mantra or a quote to guide us during seasons of uncertainty or even daily words that keep us on the right path in life. It is with these things in mind that this book was born. So, read and incorporate these wise sayings into your everyday life for more zeal and fulfillment in every aspect of your life..

Dr. Laron Matthews PhD.

POWERFUL QUOTES

1. *"You are more feared being silent around your enemies than talking around your friends"*

    DR. Laron Matthews, PhD

The people closest to you will never take you seriously. They've known everything about you, from your weaknesses and shame to your failures. So, it's harder to believe what you say or tell them to do.

But enemies who don't know you will always see you as a mystery. They'll pay attention to uncover your plans or understand who you are, to no avail. Your silence becomes your power.

So, don't be disappointed when friends don't respect you. You're more feared for being silent around your enemy than your friends you talk with freely.

Consider **Proverbs 17:28** *"Even a fool who keeps silent is considered wise; when he closes his lips, he is deemed intelligent."*

> **2.** *"When you know your history, you will know your destiny and will not serve other deities."*
>
> DR. Laron Matthews, PhD

Living without tracing your history is tantamount to wrong choices and terrible decisions. Knowing your past will uncover many reasons for the things happening in your life. Consider **Ecclesiastics 3:15** *"That which hath been is now; and that which is to be hath already been; and God requireth that which is past."*

This is why we often see history repeating itself. That's because someone failed to trace his/her pasts to uncover what could likely take place if not corrected. When you understand where you're coming from, it will be easier to choose the right path.

> **3.** *"Our enemies don't want to be revealed, but they will be exposed; Judas always comes before Justice. Be careful, he's still among the crowd and among many of us."*
>
> DR. Laron Matthews, PhD

Live carefully because the enemy of the believer doesn't rest **Ephesians 5:15**. He is still lurking around us in the shadows, waiting for the worst moment to strike. Sometimes, he uses even the most trusted people around you to carry out his deeds.

Satan is the accuser of brethren **Revelation 12:10**. He manifests physically through the vessels of dishonor. So, don't relax, and don't relent in your pursuit of justice. God will surely fight the battle to victory *2 Chronicles 20:15*.

> **4.** *"Never explain your age. Wisdom will always define your destiny in a time when you never answer from a challenging situation or person that creates a conflict to embarrass your experience."*
>
> DR Laron Matthews, PhD

Most times in life, age makes no difference in situations, but your wisdom does. Great application of wisdom will differentiate your life, making your destiny a mystery before the eyes of your challengers.

Though age will influence your decisions in difficult situations, wisdom will redefine your clear path through your numerous experiences.

Consider **Psalm 90:12** "So teach us to number our days, that we may apply our hearts unto wisdom."

> **5.** *"Everyone is not assigned to your ear, so he who controls your hearing controls your future and delays destiny thoughts about the master purpose in you."*
>
> DR Laron Mathews, PhD

Your ear, though a sensory organ, is one of the powerful tools to assimilate information that can turn your life around forever. Whomever you incline your ears will control your life and destiny.

Consider **Romans 10:17** "So then faith *cometh* by hearing, and hearing by the word of God."

Just like you will receive faith by hearing the word of God, you can also receive fear, hate, and other negativities through what you hear.

Consider **Jeremiah 29:11** "For I know the thoughts that I think toward you, saith the LORD, thoughts of peace, and not of evil, to give you an expected end."

God has a great thought for you. His purpose will act out well to ensure that you have an expected end when you incline your ears to Him and His words.

> **6.** *"You don't need money to kill a demon, you need an idea to destroy his plans."*
>
> *DR Laron Matthews, PhD*

Demons are not physical beings that you can physically fight with tools like guns, swords, axes, and other weapons your money can buy. The war against a demon is a spiritual one.

But, just like every other type of war, your spiritual war requires great strategies and outstanding ideas to help you win the fight.

Consider **1 Peter 5:8** "Be sober, be vigilant; because your adversary the devil, as a roaring lion, walketh about, seeking whom he may devour."

You must be tactful and alert to create the right idea that will help you to overcome your enemies. **Matthew 9:35-38**

> **7.** *"When you're a carrier of the promises of God, you have to deal with major persecution from the plans of your haters."*
>
> DR Laron Matthews, PhD

Satan doesn't attack anyone that is empty or has little potential in him. He moves against the mighty carriers of greatness through numerous oppositions, persecutions, and afflictions.

So, as a carrier of God's promises, you will get many oppositions and persecutions. Some people will even hate you for no just reason. But you must never relent.

Consider **Psalms 34:19** "Many *are* the afflictions of the righteous: but the LORD delivereth him out of them all."

Matthew 27-32

> **8.** *"Be careful in making bad decisions in a stressful time, they will alter your miracle when destiny shows up."*
>
> DR Laron Matthews, PhD

The decisions you make today, whether good or bad, shape your future and destiny. You must avoid reacting according to intense situations without properly analyzing the implications of your actions.

Consider **Genesis 16:1-6** "Now Sarai Abram's wife bare him no children: and she had a handmaid, an Egyptian, whose name was Hagar.

And Sarai said unto Abram, Behold now, the LORD hath restrained me from bearing: I pray thee, go in unto my maid; it may be that I may obtain children by her. And Abram hearkened to the voice of Sarai.

And Sarai Abram's wife took Hagar her maid the Egyptian, after Abram had dwelt ten years in the land of Canaan, and gave her to her husband Abram to be his wife.

And he went in unto Hagar, and she conceived: and when she saw that she had conceived, her mistress was despised in her eyes.

And Sarai said unto Abram, My wrong be upon thee: I have given my maid into thy bosom; and when she saw that she had conceived, I was despised in her eyes: the LORD judge between me and thee.

But Abram said unto Sarai, Behold, thy maid is in thine hand; do to her as it pleaseth thee. And when Sarai dealt hardly with her, she fled from her face."

Sarah's decision for her maid to sleep with her husband Abraham to conceive and bear a child became a means for the maid to torment her.

It doesn't matter who is involved, bad decisions can distort your future miracles and bring disdain to your destiny.

> **9.** *"Never underestimate the sound of jealousy in the midst of promising times. You must work to defeat failure in your mind and release disappointment from your heart."*
>
> DR Laron Matthews, PhD

There are usually experiences of jealousy at some point in our lives. However, it could be very risky to underestimate its impact once the feeling intensifies. With irrationality, jealousy could result in distrust, abuse, paranoia, or violence.

Work to avoid the jealousy around and within you, too. Jealousy can do you harm and can also make you lose focus when it's stemming from you. So, watch out and control some of its early signs like criticism, blames, hatred, fault finding, obsessive behavior, distrust, and others.

Consider **Genesis 37:5** "Then Joseph had a dream, and when he told it to his brothers, they hated him even more."

> **10.** *"Anytime you change the dynamic of a community's destiny and vision without the community's knowledge or consent, people become oppressed, losing value to their greatness."*
>
> DR Laron Matthews, PhD

Though change remains a constant process, the dynamic of a community's destiny and vision follows a contextual flow that should not easily be altered. By altering the sequential flow, the community will experience inconsistency and disorderliness in the operations of things.

Such a system will malign its citizens from their normal lives, which can cause oppression, but the bottom line is that people will never speak well of the initiator of the change. So, it destroys any good record that you might have built in the past. **Exodus 9:1**

> **11.** *Parental law kicks in when the child shows up, not by the seed of the man or the egg of the woman but when love shows out."*
>
> *DR Laron Matthews, PhD*

Nobody can become a parent without the existence of a child. That you have the natural endowment to give birth does give you any child until you produce one. Only then will your responsibility as a parent start.

This means that you must follow the sequential flow of things in every aspect of your life. Having the ability to do a thing without actually doing it is completely different.

> **12.** *"Don't allow the condition of the world to become a tradition in your life, causing you to become addicted to their ideas."*
>
> *DR Laron Matthews, PhD*

You should define a strong pattern for your life and not be easily moved around by the trend of life. Being tossed about by every opinion or lifestyle swallows your personality and identity.

Consider **1 John 2:15** "Love not the world, neither the things *that are* in the world. If any man love the world, the love of the Father is not in him."

You will always be distracted when you start having a strong affinity for trending things. Also, it creates an addiction in your life that takes you away from your original flow.

> **13.** *"When you don't do the right things, you pay the wrong price; it's called high price of low living."*
>
> *DR Laron Matthews, PhD*

Every action you take has a sequential reaction that follows you. Making wrong moves brews negative influences and impacts on your life. Some of the consequences could either be immediate or in the future.

Consider **Galatians 6:7** "Be not deceived; God is not mocked: for whatsoever a man soweth, that shall he also reap."

You must remember that there's a price for everything you do. God has made the natural laws that you will reap whatever you sow.

> **14.** *God's promotion is not a punishment; it is power telling pressure you must graduate before you burst."*
>
> *DR Laron Matthews, PhD*

God is not an author of confusion in His children's lives. When He lifts a man, it's for a purpose and the person must measure up to what God has in store for him.

You must have what it takes to be at a certain level for God to take you there. He may not be focusing on outward appearance and abilities as men do.

Consider **Proverbs 10:22** "The blessing of the LORD, it maketh rich, and he addeth no sorrow with it."

So, when God decides to promote you, it's not a form of punishment. He has seen what you can do and there will be no regrets for God's position in your life.

> **15.** *"If you can't heal right, you can't love right; well, love wins again."*
>
> *DR Laron Matthews, PhD*

What you have is what you can give. You can take out what isn't within you. You can reproduce or present love to others where you don't have love.

It takes a man who is completely whole within him to love completely without reservation. When you are hurting within yourself, it will be impossible to love. There's a need for you to heal from within in order to produce pure love that can be felt.

> **16.** *"Don't kill people with your strength and don't destroy them with your weakness."*
>
> DR Laron Matthews, PhD

Your life shouldn't be a discouragement or destruction to others. You should consider both the strengths and weaknesses of people in your dealings. Some individuals could be intimidated by your capabilities. Also, some people could get discouraged due to your lack of commitment and unseriousness in some cases.

In circumstances where lots of people look up to you as a role model, your intentional flaws could destroy most of their ideologies about life. This means that you have unintentionally contributed to building negative concepts in the lives of such one.

You must ensure that your actions or even inactions are not either intimidation or destruction to others.

Consider **Hebrews 12:**1 "Wherefore seeing we also are compassed about with so great a cloud of witnesses, let us lay aside every weight, and the sin which doth so easily beset *us*, and let us run with patience the race that is set before us,"

> **17.** *"Whatever you do, you must test positive for faith, negative for sin, faith cometh by hearing, sin comes by falling. Stand tall and hear from the Lord."*
>
> DR Laron Matthews, PhD

Your faith in God is a great tool that pushes you higher both with Him and in life. When you start doubting, you will start falling and that leads you to sin.

Consider **Romans 10:17** "So then faith *cometh* by hearing, and hearing by the word of God."

Build your life to depend on the word of God. It's His word that develops the faith and hope that will carry you through the storms of life. When you surround yourself with negative news and influences, you will easily slip into sin. Stand out for God and prove your faith in Him.

> **18.** *"You must be willing to disciple your own mind and thoughts during a stressful time and emotional hours. They determine your 'destiny sound.'"*
>
> DR Laron Matthews, PhD

Discipling is a unique virtue that cultivates self-control and excellence. It follows the traits that your attitude will determine your altitude.

By drilling your mind and thoughts through discipline, especially during difficult times, you can fashion your destiny to great success.

Knowing how to control and manage your tough emotional periods is the right key to progressive advancement in life. See **Galatians 5:22-23.**

> **19.** *"In the midst of being a flawed person, greatness in God is about to overtake you for His purpose."*
>
> *DR Laron Matthews, PhD*

You are never the same once you give your life to Christ. Irrespective of the sins you've committed in the past, the power of God will overtake all in your life.

Consider **2 Corinthians 5:17** "Therefore if any man be in Christ, he is a new creature: old things are passed away; behold, all things are become new."

There's a complete change that happens with your personality. God's greatness overtakes you and all about you changes according to His purpose.

> **20.** *"God is getting ready to market you before the enemy make a mockery of you."*
>
> *DR Laron Matthews, PhD*

You are never out of God's thoughts and plans. He has a bigger picture for you. He wants to announce you to the world, and the enemy has no chance of executing his evil acts over you.

Consider **Jeremiah 29:11** "For I know the thoughts that I think toward you, saith the LORD, thoughts of peace, and not of evil, to give you an expected end."

God's publicity is the best thing that could happen to any life. It removes reproach and places you before those who matter in society.

> **21.** *"Your future is getting ready to shine so bright you have to give your enemies shades so they won't be blinded by your blessing."*
>
> *DR Laron Matthews, PhD*

You must understand the personality God has made you to be. You are destined for greatness and no power of your enemies can stop you. You will shine so bright that those who never believed in you will be amazed at who you've become.

Consider **Isaiah 60: 1** "Arise, shine; for thy light is come, and the glory of the LORD is risen upon thee."

The glory of God is upon you and nothing can stop your manifestation.

> **22.** *"People can take your stuff, but they can't take your favor. Favor will follow you for the rest of your life."*
>
> *DR Laron Matthews, PhD*

The Lord has laid a great path that opens unlimited favor for you. It doesn't matter if people plan on frustrating your life; you won't go down.

Though they may take your stuff, your entitlement, your rights, or even delay your promotions, it's just temporary. You are truly unstoppable and the set time for your manifestation will take you to your favor.

Consider **Psalms 102:13** "Thou shalt arise, and have mercy upon Zion: for the time to favour her, yea, the set time, is come."

> **23.** *People are working so hard for an empty space that doesn't exist in eternity only in time, leaving them in a voided situation and painful memories*
>
> *DR Laron Matthews, PhD*

You must understand how and where to direct your energy while you still have the time. When you live outside God's fold, you are wasting your time for irrelevant purposes that will affect your eternity negatively.

Consider **Mark 8:36** "For what shall it profit a man, if he shall gain the whole world, and lose his own soul?"

When you focus on world pursuit and neglect to prepare your soul for a great eternity, you will just end up with regrets in the future. Remember that you have no gain when you enjoy this life but put your soul to eternal damnation.

> **24.** *"Your obedience to God is a down payment, but many people don't want to be on His payroll."*
>
> *DR Laron Matthews, PhD*

God cherishes obedience beyond everything. Your obedience to God covers everything in your relationship. This depicts your total surrender and faith in Him, which is the only thing that could move God.

Consider **1 Samuel 15:22** "And Samuel said, Hath the LORD *as great* delight in burnt offerings and sacrifices, as in obeying the voice of the LORD? Behold, to obey *is* better than sacrifice, *and* to hearken than the fat of rams."

Your obedience is the key to receiving everything from God. He values your obedience more than whatever else you could offer.

Consider **Romans 4:3** "For what saith the scripture? Abraham believed God, and it was counted unto him for righteousness."

> **25.** *"When your purpose passes your potential, your enemies are always in trouble, period."*
>
> *DR Laron Matthews, PhD*

The purpose is what keeps you in line with your destiny. When you keep walking on your purpose, it's a sure way to fulfill your destiny.

Living according to your purpose requires the application of your potential. So, your purpose is the driving force for your potential. Being focused on your purpose remains a mystery to your enemies. With greater purpose, your enemies can never understand or predict your moves.

> **26.** *"If you watch your mind, it will watch your mouth. Out of the abundance of the heart, the mouth speaks. Watch your mind, it will protect your life destiny."*
>
> DR Laron Matthews, PhD

Your personality has a strong link with what your mind processes. Your mind is the source of what comes out both from your mouth and your attitude.

If you must go far in life, you need to control the reasoning of your mind. This is because it controls your destiny.

Consider **Proverbs 4:23** "Keep thy heart with all diligence; for out of it *are* the issues of life."

You should guide what you feed your heart and your mind with. This determines how your life will turn out.

> **27.** *"Whatever you do in life, don't put yourself under stresses that don't qualify for your destiny."*
>
> DR Laron Matthews, PhD

Not everything or activity matters in life. You should avoid trying to engage in things that stress you. Anything that has no contributory role in your destiny is a waste of energy and resources.

Learn to live for things that add positive influence to you. Creating unnecessary stress will break you down and cut off your destiny.

Consider **Phil 4:8** "Finally, brethren, whatsoever things are true, whatsoever things *are* honest, whatsoever things *are* just, whatsoever things *are* pure, whatsoever things *are* lovely, whatsoever things *are* of good report; if *there be* any virtue, and if *there be* any praise, think on these things."

Always remember that stress is a killer. Keep your life's flow very simple.

> **28.** *"The closer you get to God, the less the cares of life becomes, and the power of God is manifested in you and through you."*
>
> *DR Laron Matthews, PhD*

Whatever or wherever you pay more attention will become the principal focus of life. When you get closer to God, it takes your eyes and minds away from the issues and worries in life. It activates the fullness of God's power in your life.

Consider **James 4:8** "Draw nigh to God, and he will draw nigh to you. Cleanse *your* hands, *ye* sinners; and purify *your* hearts, *ye* double minded."

Once you start moving closer to God, He will also move closer to you. This opens His unlimited power in you and through you.

> **29.** *"When you are in a world filled with people that make assumptions, one must be able to value wisdom and apply it to understanding."*
>
> *DR Laron Matthews, PhD*

Though you are in the world, you are not of the world. The assumptions and wicked imaginations of evil people should not be your standard of living.

You must differentiate yourself through God's wisdom. With the application of God's understanding, you will be able to stand out among others.

Consider **Proverbs 2:1-4** "My son, if thou wilt receive my words, and hide my commandments with thee;

So that thou incline thine ear unto wisdom, and apply thine heart to understanding;

Yea, if thou criest after knowledge, and liftest up thy voice for understanding;

If thou seekest her as silver, and searchest for her as for hid treasures;"

> **30.** *"When destiny is in your belly, it will restore damage from people's lives."*
>
> *DR Laron Matthews, PhD*

Your life doesn't depend on the activities and plans of your enemies. When you understand who you are in Christ and live to fulfill your destiny, it will keep you far above the devices and works of your enemies. Afterall "No weapon formed against you shall prosper."

Consider **Job 5:12** "He disappointeth the devices of the crafty, so that their hands cannot perform *their* enterprise."

Keeping yourself fully in God disgraces the devices of your enemies. There will be a complete restoration of your destiny.

> **31.** *"You're being trained by your enemies but promoted by God."*
>
> DR Laron Matthews, PhD

The troubles and trials you encounter in life due to the enemy's assignment against you, often serves as a catalyst to forge character and strength within you. Gold must be tried in fire to remove its impurity and bring it to its purest state. Enemy fire becomes a training ground to make your faith stronger. While your enemies are on one side training you to be stronger through travails, God is on the other side elevating you to greatness.

See Jeremiah 29: 11 For I know the plans I have for you, declares the Lord. Plans to prosper you and not to harm you. Plans to give you hope and a future.

Consider **Psalms 75:6-7** "For promotion *cometh* neither from the east, nor from the west, nor from the south.

But God *is* the Judge: He puts down one, And exalts another."

> **32.** *"Love has a rhythm that is far greater than the anatomy of two people coming together to experience each other. It's called oneness, "the covenant."*
>
> DR Laron Matthews, PhD

The act of love has a pattern of its own. This pattern is much more than the joining of two people who want to explore their sexuality. Love makes two different people unite and become one person in mind and soul. It is like an agreement to unite. **See Deuteronomy 6: 4 - 5**

---

33. *"Jesus finished the sound and gave us the frequency."*

DR Laron Matthews, PhD

In our walk with Christ, we are not the ones that complete the principal work of redemption. Jesus accomplished that on the cross of Calvary. It is through His finished work that we inherit the frequency of eternity to govern this earth realm.

Consider **Revelations 12:11** "And they overcame him by the blood of the Lamb, and by the word of their testimony; and they loved not their lives unto the death."

---

34. *"The unknown is mystery's greatest friend and power to those to whom the secrets are revealed."*

DR Laron Matthews, PhD

Whatever you don't know in life will remain a mystery to you. It puts you in a state of confusion and can even create fear within you.

But for those with knowledge, it becomes a strong and powerful weapon. Discovering the unknown among those who are still in ignorance gives you insight and places you in a position of authority.

Always strive to acquire wisdom and knowledge that will bring illumination and keep you walking in wisdom.

Proverbs 25:2 It is the glory of God to conceal a thing but the honor of kings is to search out a matter.

Consider **Proverbs 4:7** "Wisdom *is* the principal thing; *therefore* get wisdom: and with all thy getting get understanding."

> **35.** *"When you see a person with cracks in their lives, it's not the drugs they're on, it's the cracks in their heart and the painful thoughts of their past."*
>
> *DR Laron Matthews, PhD*

When we fail to address the trauma and pains that have left fractures in our souls and we observe cycles of destructive behaviors, don't think it's a result of sin rather the result of unaddressed pain.

> **36.** *"The issue is not policing, racism, injustice or hate. The issue is the world has defunded "love" and devalued human life."*
>
> *DR Laron Matthews, PhD*

The problem humanity is facing is not because we are restricted, discriminated against, or despised. The problem is that the world has withdrawn from "love" and treats human life lightly.

> **37.** *"Fear never gives faith the opportunity to reveal life's true secret of you in you."*
>
> DR Laron Matthews, PhD

Fear is a destroyer. It's false evidence appearing to be real. It consumes your self-confidence and consistently brings a feeling of doubt in your mind. You will never believe in yourself when you enslave your heart with fear.

Your true abilities and potential will only manifest when you have faith in yourself. You will be amazed at the great strength and accomplishment you can achieve with faith. This could only happen when you remove fear.

Consider **2 Timothy 1:7** "For God hath not given us the spirit of fear; but of power, and of love, and of a sound mind."

Remember that fear doesn't exist with faith. Move with the spirit of a sound mind and release your great potential from within.

> **38.** *"The unknown is mystery's greatest friend and power to them who knows themselves"*
>
> DR Laron Matthews, PhD

Anything you do not know about is just like an enigma or puzzle to you. But if you can understand it, the knowledge will give you power.

> **39.** *"Many people never experience marriage, they experience what flesh want to marry."*
>
> DR Laron Matthews, PhD

Due to the wrong decisions most people make when they are going into marriage, it becomes difficult for them to benefit from the joys of marriage. They didn't ask for God's will when choosing their life partner. Instead, they chose their life partners according to their likes and wants. As a result, their experience in marriage will never be what it is destined to be but what they orchestrated for themselves. As a Christian, you shouldn't work by sight but by faith. See **2 Cor. 5:7** "For we walk by faith, not by sight."

> **40.** *The reason why the millionaires are so poor is they seek after money and never embrace wealth."*
>
> DR Laron Matthews, PhD

Millionaires are so rich in money and the things of the world. But they lack the most important thing, which is the spiritual wealth that comes from God.

They believe that they have everything but do not know that they are very poor in the things that matter most. Without God in their lives, whatever they have is worthless, thus rendering them poor. See **Luke 12:20** "But God said unto him, *Thou* fool, this night thy soul shall be required of thee: then whose shall those things be, which thou hast provided?"

> **41.** *"I can deal with a person with a struggle but not a habit; a struggle will make you cry, a habit will cause death."*
>
> *DR Laron Matthews, PhD*

It is easier to help someone who still has a conscience. When he/she is doing badly, he/she can still feel regret with the knowledge that what they are doing is not right. But anyone who has formed doing evil as a habit believes that it is another way of life. Such a person cannot be saved and will commit evil until the day of his/her life. See **Rom. 6: 23.**

> **42.** *"Patience will always be the masterpiece to a great victory in all champions."*
>
> *DR Laron Matthews, PhD*

To any person who exercises patience, victory will be your great reward. Check the story of those who gained victory over travesty in the Bible like Job. He became victorious at the end because he patiently waited upon the Lord. See **Lamentations 3: 25.**

> **43.** *"Love is a story that can be written without a book being present."*
>
> *DR Laron Matthews, PhD*

Love is a natural emotion that comes to someone. You don't need to be taught by someone how to love. It comes directly from your heart without rules of engagement. Once you have God in you, love will automatically flow through you because he is love. See **1 Cor. 13: 4-5 & Songs of Solomon 8:7.**

> **44.** *"Don't allow people to tell your story from their feel-good moment and others conversational piece. You tell your story from your pains, and your experiment will write life's best seller, "The You."*
>
> *DR Laron Matthews, PhD*

It is not good to allow others to tell the story of your life. They will tell you favorable bits about you when they are in a good mood. And at other times, they use you as a source of entertainment. That is why you should explain yourself better through your life experiences. Speak out through your pains and joys. People will understand you better.

> **45.** *"When you create what you want for your future to be outside of the Creator, you establish an allusion that will get you nowhere in life but on an island in your mind. Void of understanding and never take you anywhere."*
>
> *DR Laron Matthews, PhD*

If you plan your life without God, you are making a great mistake. What you are doing is hinting at life that will never take you anywhere except to your fantasy world. When you do not understand the will of God for your life, you will never achieve the destiny preordained for you by God. See **Hosea 4: 6.**

> **46.** *"Don't allow people's personal feelings to stop you from the opportunity greatness will present to you from within destiny chambers of your soul."*
>
> *DR Laron Matthews, PhD*

People will always share their opinions about things based on their emotions, perceptions or experiences. Instead of basing your decisions on these feelings of others, why not believe in yourself and act based on your own feelings and perceptions? Don't let other people's emotions hinder you from grabbing your chance of greatness. They will communicate their fears and unbelief to you and discourage you. Instead, listen and believe the call to greatness from your soul.

> **47.** *"When you walk in creation, you don't worry about human citizenship, which means documentation to the world. When you become a creation, the Creator gives you power that comes from eternity and responds to the universe, and releases the mysteries of the Creator's blueprint in the earth realm that will open up the vaults of human wisdom."*
>
> *DR Laron Matthews, PhD*

Being a God's child is better than being recognized by the world. Even if you're unimportant in the eyes of men right now, don't bother yourself. Trust God and keep His ways, He'll equip you with the knowledge you need to live better and even understand the mysteries of the world. So, focus on Him alone, and you'll not go astray. See **Proverbs 3 5-6.**

> **48.** *"True love is not in it for the time, it's in it for eternity; in every man and woman on earth, there is a place in you called eternity. It's next to the place called internal conflict, the only battle is external things, the greatest love is eternal"*
>
> DR Laron Matthews, PhD

Never allow yourself to miss out on a great opportunity to become someone in life because of the fear of what people will say about you. When you do good deeds, people will talk about you. Likewise, people will still talk about you when you do bad things. So take your chance when you see it and fight for everlasting things.

> **49.** *"If you ever want to find the enemies, search for them in the deepest part of you where you gave them freedom and see, where you altered destiny, and your love will change the course and create a classic moment."*
>
> DR Laron Matthews, PhD

The enemies you are looking for are never far from you. They are those who you see and interact with every day of your life. Unknown to you, you allowed them to gain access to you and change the course of your life. However, due to your selfless love that accommodates all, God will look upon it and change your destiny back to its expected glorious end.

> **50.** *"If you don't deal with the truth, you lose moral authority; if you allow in the land immorality, you cause morality to run. It's time for moral people to take a stand and stop acting like they are on their knees when many have sold their soul to a demonic system in the land."*
>
> *DR Laron Matthews, PhD*

If you are one of those that is always in denial and never faces the truth because of how horrible it is, you are likely to forget your moral standard.

By doing so, you are allowing evil to flood the land. Now is the right time for the righteous ones to stand firm and stop compromising with immorality. Especially now that many people have compromised with their moral authority in the land.

See **Rom. 3:23**

> **51.** *"Pain" is where I was, "promise" is where I'm at, "power" is where I stand, "purpose" is what I have, and God is all I need."*
>
> *DR Laron Matthews, PhD*

I was in a difficult position, but I believed in God's promises, which gave me the power to hold steadfast to my objective. God is the only one I ever needed.

See **Matt. 17: 20.**

> **52.** *"They say time sits still but the reality is your destiny is being held up because you are a diamond carrier of the presence of eternity."*
>
> DR Laron Matthews, PhD

The truth of the matter is that time never stands still. What remains the same no matter when it comes to actualization is your destiny. Your destiny can be delayed, but it can never be denied. The enemies will always try their best to hinder your progress because you are a carrier of greatness. See **Daniel 10:13.**

> **53.** *"Back in the day, that's another story; now, history knows our anointing; no matter how many chapters people tell from the old pages of your books, it's a best seller in the eyes of God "now.""*
>
> DR Laron Matthews, PhD

Your former life is one thing. But presently, history is aware of you and your capabilities. So, no matter how eloquent people are in discussing your past misdeeds, everything is right in the eyes of God. For those who are in Christ, you are a new creature, old things have passed away, and everything has become new.

See **2 Cor. 5:17.**

> **54.** *"When deity (God) meets damage (you), your destiny emerges into a great kingdom gift for him; get ready you for a kingdom turnaround now."*
>
> *DR Laron Matthews, PhD*

When God comes across a damaged person being you, He makes your destiny explode in a great way. And through such a miracle, His name will be glorified. So, prepare yourself to receive a divine turnaround right now.

> **55.** *"Faith is an enemy of fear, and because faith comes by hearing and hearing by the word of God, let faith control your hearing and your sound will defeat the enemies."*
>
> *DR Laron Matthews, PhD*

Fear can never work together with faith. All you need to forget fear and embrace faith is the word of God.

Don't listen to the fears of others around you. Always read your bible and listen to faith-filled words from powerful men of God. By so doing, you will not fall prey to the predator who wants you to lose your faith in God. See **Hebrews 11:6**

56. *"Obedience comes with a price, but it's surely a down payment for your next blessing and the promises that can't be stopped."*

DR Laron Matthews, PhD

Being obedient to God must cost you something. But no matter whatever price you pay in the service of God, it is never in vain. Regard it as your insurance to the blessings of the Lord as well as His unending promises.

57. *"You will never have a resolution without a revolution. The prophetic showdown is in motion, leaders transitioning into the new posture with the paradigm sound that will destroy the generational pathology of the enemy's plans against mankind and God's remnant that are emerging now. We are an unstoppable sound in the earth realms now "israel13.""*

DR Laron Matthews, PhD

You shouldn't be surprised by everything happening in the world today. There is no way a resolution will take place without an uprising. Everything will work out in the end to favor those who truly believe in God. Even in the midst of all these turbulent times, believe and trust God because all things are working together to achieve God's purpose for his children. See **Romans 8:28.**

58. *"All-points bulletin in the earth realm, many of you are pregnant right now and you're about to deliver; however, there's a wind called abortion, i.e. (Distractors) against your prophetic babies in the earth realms in "you."*

DR Laron Matthews, PhD

Many people are carriers of great messages that can change the world. God has equipped you with amazing gifts and talents to evangelize for Him. However, there are distractors everywhere who are working against you. They don't want you to deliver prophecies in you to the world. Be mindful of these distractors and refocus on what the Lord has packaged you to do.

59. *"Whatever you do, don't allow your past issue to stop your future endeavor "destiny.""*

DR Laron Matthews, PhD

The devil is always reminding us of our past mistakes, thereby limiting and stagnating us with fear. No matter whatever is happening around you, never allow your past mistakes to hinder you from achieving your future goals or destiny. Don't feed the fear from the devil. Instead, overcome him by the words of your testimony.

See **Revelation 12: 11**.

> **60.** *"The kingdom of God has not made it hard for the people. It's people from the so-called kingdom that has made it hard for "us" to stop making people Gods and iconic but make the word authentic so the truth can prevail."*
>
> *DR Laron Matthews, PhD*

The kingdom of heaven made it very easy for us all to enter through our Lord Jesus Christ, who came to die for our sins. We only need to believe in Him and accept Him as our Lord and personal Savior. See **John 3:16**. However, it is the leaders of the earthly realm that are making the kingdom of heaven very difficult for the people of God. Desist from enthroning people to become majestic. Instead, make the word of God genuine so that the truth can triumph.

> **61.** *"In this season of ministries, your sound must be just as great as to touch, and your view must be just as powerful as a look destiny phantom your love in how you deal with my time and my pains."*
>
> *DR Laron Matthews, PhD*
>
> **62.** *"I'm no longer a slave to fear but I am a child of God."*

Once you are a child of God, fear will no longer have any power over you. Your trust will be centered on God, who is able to perform all things. When He who is with you is more powerful than he who is in the world, there's no reason to fear. See **2Timothy 1:7**.

63. *This is for someone right "now," stop listening to greedy leaders who want to seize the moment after your painful season; your pains are about to bless you with wealth uncommon to men's bank accounts "now."*

DR Laron Matthews, PhD

Do not mind the things happening around you. Focus on God and believe that things will turn out for the best. Every painful experience you have passed through will prepare you for the uncommon wealth that no one can understand.

64. *"It's your season to know; faith is a refusal to panic, in a demonic pandemic."*

DR Laron Matthews, PhD

Faith makes you see things beyond the visible. When others are panicking about the immediate things, your faith in God tells you that all things work together for good to them that love God. So, now is the right time to know that having faith means that you have refused to feel fear in this devilish pandemic.

65. *"Get ready something good is about to transpire-in your life, something that has happened to you, and your enemies can't stop it "now.""*

DR Laron Matthews, PhD

We face lots of challenges every day. Sometimes, they're so painful that you might think it's all over. But do you know that God can change things for you? He can even make a way in the wilderness. So, trust Him and prepare yourself now to accept the blessings of the Lord that are coming your way. The blessings you will receive, no man or enemy can stop it. See **Isaiah 43: 19**

> **66.** *"You must move at the sound of a deity even though you live in the place of humanity."*
>
> DR Laron Matthews, PhD

Walking by the direction of God is better than moving according to men's seasons and plans. So, endeavor to make a move any time you hear the voice of God. Allow the divine to direct your way even though you're still here on earth.

> **67.** *"As a leader, you have to stay at the feet of the Father to get answers for the people's needs, cries, pains, hurts, and even this virus that's dominating the earth realms through people's minds."*
>
> DR Laron Matthews, PhD

If you want to be a good leader, you need to humble yourself to God. That is the only way you can receive the answers to your people's needs, cries, pains, hurts, and even the antidote to the prevailing disease that has psychologically dominated the earth's realms.

See **2Chro. 1:-11-12.**

> **68.** *"Your anointing is about to destroy these enemies in your atmospheric realms called viruses and there are many and they are legions."*
>
> *DR Laron Matthews, PhD*

The divine touch upon your life is going to wreak havoc upon your enemies in the earthly realms. It doesn't matter the things happening around you or the issues facing the world. The anointing of God upon your life will make a difference and protect you against the evil permeating human existence.

> **69.** *"I decree God's will be done from heaven, that your purpose shall be manifested in the earth realms."*
>
> *DR Laron Matthews, PhD*

I proclaim that the will of God will be done from heaven. Also, God's purpose should be established on earth.

> **70.** *"Whatever you do, make peace with your past and past people so that conversation doesn't hinder your future manifestation from God and your present victory. You're getting ready to walk into the now in your life."*
>
> *DR Laron Matthews, PhD*

In every one of your undertakings, always make sure that you are at peace with everything and everyone that affected your life in the past. That is to make sure that nothing prevents the future manifestations coming to you from God as well as your imminent victory.

> **71.** *"Great season of blessing will know your name, great season of opportunity will know your destiny."*
>
> *DR Laron Matthews, PhD*

You're set for good things. The blessings of God are for His people, and you won't be left out. God will make opportunities to come your way and announce your destiny for you.

> **72.** *"Whatever you do today, allow love to return home and have its rightful place in your heart.....God told David he was a man after my own heart, the heart carries many untold love secrets from God.....search the heart you will find many secrets and they will keep you sacred...Love the Unfinished Chapter- 2016..".*

In everything you may do in life, let love take the position it is supposed to take within your heart. The heart of man contains a great number of untold love mysteries from God. God is love and He dwells in you. That means you're a carrier of divine love. Don't give room for anything else so that the love within you will reign.

73. *"Are you in kingdom covenant or church contracts".....*
the Kingdom of God is consistent with covenant and
not contract, the Kingdom of God is not about the
contract but it's about covenant. We have too many
people operating only under contracts and no covenant,
a covenant will not be broken neither change nor
altered, real kingdom leaders strengthen truth, correct
sins, restore error and build kingdom men and women
of God back to the kingdom imagery without destroying
their character, which equal priestly royalty in the
Kingdom of God, that is why the kingdom divided
against itself cannot stand, kingdom leader, let's stand
together for the Kingdom of God."

Ask yourself this question: Are you in a covenant with God or under
a contract with the church? God's kingdom works well together
with covenants and not with contracts. The Kingdom of God is
not all about arrangements that you may have with the church
authorities. Instead, it is all about your pact or treaty with God.
Yet, many Christians today work under an arrangement in the
house of God instead of the pact they have with Almighty God.
What they don't know is that any covenant with God can never be
broken or changed. In contrast, a contract can be altered, changed,
or broken. The real men of God nourish truth, correct sin, restore
mistakes, and raise kingdom men and women. Bringing them
back to the divine vision without damaging their character which
is similar to priestly royalty in God's kingdom. That is what the

Bible said: Any kingdom divided against itself cannot stand. See Matt. 12:25. Thus, rulers of the kingdom, let us all work together with each other for the Kingdom of God.

> **74.** *"People want you to live life out of their own book that they will not follow, themselves."*
>
> DR Laron Matthews, PhD

Most people are so quick to give advice, rules, and regulations—even specifications—they don't live by. In fact, most humans provide unrealistic expectations for others to live by, whereas they disregard these set expectations. Hypocrisy is, at best, a sour mindset of hypocrites.

They will tell you how you should live your life to be perfect, but they will never lead that same way. So, don't ever believe what others say is right, but seek counsel from the Holy Spirit within you. He will guide you in all things. See **John 16:13.**

> **75.** *"When you have an encounter with wisdom, your experience will look like a joke."*
>
> DR Laron Matthews, PhD

Wisdom is readily available to anyone who cares well enough to focus on it (Proverbs 8:1-5). Wisdom transforms a man inside-out; from his thoughts to actions, every encounter with wisdom slowly transforms a man's life.

Also, it's important to notice that the result of wisdom doesn't happen overnight. It's a gradual process. But, every spiritual encounter with the scriptures becomes more simplified and life's experiences become more directional.

> **76.** *"Get ready for the pursuit of destiny in the season of the triangle of love. A threesome can't work when you're the 'One in a million' in the heart of God."*
>
> *DR Laron Matthews, PhD*

When you're chasing after God, get ready for a change of a lifetime. Remember, it's a personal relationship with God, not congregational. It's not a group; it's you and God.

So, while on your journey with God, ensure to drop every form of distraction and prioritize God. He loves you so much that He says, "Draw closer to me and I will draw closer to you." (James 4:8).

> **77.** *"Every computer that has been hacked has been hacked by a virus or someone that wants your data. You find the hacker, you close the case, you find the virus, you fix your computer. You walk in faith, you defeat fear; you apply the blood, you destroy the virus."*
>
> *DR Laron Matthews, PhD*

Any problem you are facing originates from somewhere. It may be caused by a deadly enemy or someone who wants to know all about your life to control you. When you know where your problem is coming from, you can easily block it from affecting you. Then, you find the solution to the mess it has created.

One of the most powerful weapons of the enemy is fear. Although subtle, fear comes in the form of worry, concerns, TODOs, patterns, etc. However, God provides a superior weapon for not only defeating fear but walking in constant victory—faith.

You must be careful about what you think about or permit in your mind. Also, a mighty tool for defeating the enemy is your "shield of faith." Arm yourself properly (**Ephesians 6:16-18**).

When you are walking with God, you can conquer the spirit of fear. And with the blood of Jesus, you can destroy any hidden enemy. See **Exodus: 12:13.**

> **78.** *"Is the suffering that you're going through now because of your past disobedience?"*
>
> *Mother Ellen Allen.*

Sometimes, we think that the bad experiences we're going through are because of some spiritual disfavor against us. Whereas, some of the time, it's not even about that.

Have you checked whether the agony you are passing through these days is because of your past misdeeds? Our past influences and our future. So, when things are seemingly tough, look back to know if they're a result of your sins and wrong decisions. Do this before blaming others around you.

Iniquity is doing things your own way—without regard for God (**Isaiah 53:6**). Now, iniquities bring mishaps to us. It might not be you outrightly sinning against your Maker, but not choosing to go where He sends you to or doing what He commands.

So, take some time to reconsider: is this problem you're going through because of your disobedience?

> **79.** *"Touch the like button and say 'No Pain, No Gain.'"*
>
> *Dr. Laron Matthews, Ph.D.*

If you want to accomplish something great in life, then be ready to discomfort yourself and make sacrifices. Why? Great things in life require persistence and stubborn doggedness.

As a soldier in life, expect to discomfort yourself to attain success. Are you ready for it? (**Romans 8:18**).

> **80.** *""There are many of you who are pregnant right now and you're about to deliver. However, there's a wind called abortion—i.e., distractors—against your prophetic invention, wittiness, copyright blueprint, and finally, patents that no man can stop. Press in; the heads of the babies are coming out. That's why the injustice systems (racism) put their knees on the head of a birther (Seed) who yelled 'I can't breathe.' Stay connected; everyone needs a PROPHET in their life to release the kingdom mysteries in the land."*
>
> *Dr. Laron Matthews, Ph.D.*

Everyone carries a seed, and enemies are coming to take that seed from you. God has spoken a word for your life; what is it He's said about you? You need to realize that the enemies will come in different forms to kill your seed, even if it means killing you (**1 Peter 5:8**).

> **81.** *"I want to prophesy to someone today: more people were counting on your dying than to live. But I prophesy to you today, Live! Live! Live! And now, I speak health, wealth, prosperity!"*
>
> *Dr. Laron Matthews, Ph.D.*

When you look around you today, the issues of life and enemies are only seeking your downfall and death. But the Lord has a different plan for you. He wants you to live and glorify Him. God wants you to prosper and not end in misery. All you need is to trust in Him and focus your faith on God. Then, all the good things in store for you will manifest.

There are tons of people who are waiting for you to perish. Your downfall is what they want to see. The real reason for all this is because of their inert envy that they can't deal with (**Jeremiah 17:9**). But God that has called you out of the darkness of this world will see you through.

You shall excel because the word of the Lord says so (**Daniel 6:3-4**).

> **82.** *"Destiny is always in your sound, and fear always operates from your flesh."*
>
> *Dr. Laron Matthews, Ph.D.*

Fear works on the facts of things that your eyes can see and your mind can comprehend physically. Your emotion is an attribute of the flesh. It also allows you to feel the impact within what you see without.

However, never keep quiet about your situation. Instead, shout out to the Lord with joy (**Psalm 35:27**).

> **83.** *"The world can't stop the Word; the Word of God is inside of you."*
>
> *Dr. Laron Matthews, Ph.D.*

The Word of God is the potent power of the Creator; nothing under creation can stop the word of God. However, it's only your mind that can stop the Word of God from manifesting in your life (Matthew 13: 4-7, 18-22).

Apart from that and sins, if you're in the Kingdom of God, nothing on earth, heaven, and beneath the earth can ever stop the Word of God from manifesting in your life.

> **84.** *"God is going to show your enemies that it was He that blessed you, and not them."*
>
> *Dr. Laron Matthews, Ph.D.*

The blessings of the Lord will make ways for you and not add sorrow. If the Lord has blessed you, never fear what the enemies can do. They cannot hinder your blessings or stop it from reaching you. Since God Himself championed these blessings, He will never allow their plans to work. So, the enemies cannot have the final say in your life.

It's God who blesses His beloved, and that's both you and I and everyone who is identified with Christ. God makes a man who he is (**James 4:6**). God chooses to bless whoever He wants, and when He does, there's nothing your enemies can do about it.

Get ready for the blessings of the Lord; it will come in full measure this season. Are you ready (**Psalm 23:5**)?

> **85.** *"Many people are in an identity crisis. Whomever this is for, God wants you to know that help is on the way and destiny is about to make a way."*
>
> Dr. Laron Matthews, Ph.D.

There are many people out there who find it difficult to know who they are. And they are not comfortable with such a situation. So, if you are having problems with recognizing who you are, don't worry. No matter who you may be, the Lord wants you to know that your helper is coming soon. Moreover, your destiny is on its way to fulfillment.

At the very root of your Christianity is your identity in Christ Jesus. If you don't realize your identity in Christ, you will end up in an identity crisis (**Psalm 82:5-6**). So, understand your identity in Christ: His plans, purposes, promises, etc., for you.

This way, you can easily accept the revelations of God's help from His Word.

> **86.** *"The real cost to be a leader is not in the title, it's in the gene. It comes from God's genealogy within you."*
>
> *Dr. Laron Matthews, Ph.D.*

Being a good leader is more than the title. You have to really be there for others, take important decisions, move others and achieve goals. The truth is that if you're doing well as a leader right now, it is all thanks to God's deposits of knowledge and strength in you. If you're struggling to achieve your leadership goals, ask God to empower His strength in you.

God has called you to become a light to the world (**Isaiah 60:1-4, Matthew 5:14**). As a leader, the title comes with a burden—a responsibility—you need to pay much attention to rather than focusing on the glory that comes from it. Leadership is a responsibility, not glory, not fame—but the responsibility that comes from salvation. We are saved to save others, to save the world (**Mark 16:15**).

> **87.** *"The prophetic sound is calling all remnants to the forefront now. That is why many prophetic people are in a shift in their lives in the earth realms."*
>
> *Dr. Laron Matthews, Ph.D.*

There is a high demand for the remnants of God in this earthly realm. A sound is calling out loud (**Isaiah 40:3**) for believers to join the train. When people follow the voice and instructions of a prophetic preacher, it's easier for them to enter into a series of prophetic seasons seamlessly. Follow the voice of God today (**Hebrews 3:15-17**).

> **88.** *"This is the season to study history and not 'his story.' God is greater than men's religious way. But your anointed knowledge and wisdom will open the kingdom mysteries for the people's lives."*
>
> Dr. Laron Matthews, Ph.D.

Most often, we focus on the wrong things. People try to find out God's ways for the sake of making a discovery, whereas they don't see the right things. What has God been doing in the realms of man? Why has He been doing so?

We need to stop boxing God's ways into patterns and focus on the true perspective. Instead of listening or watching the events unfolding around you in this era, why not think back to who God really is?

Everything is moving towards a different road than what it used to be. So, try to remember the olden days and everything that happened in the Bible. When you do, you will realize that God is extraordinary and much more than the rigid ways of men. However, your blessed understanding and wisdom will reveal the hidden things of the kingdom meant for His people.

> **89.** *"The abundance comes with your obedience. Then, riches will be released into your destiny."*
>
> Dr. Laron Matthews, Ph.D.

Obeying God's Word is a surefire way of gaining everything you ever want in life. God is the giver of every good thing, and without Him is nothing. So, obey God's words, keep His commandments, and He'll teach your hands to make wealth, get fulfilment and joy untold. Consider **Deuteronomy 8:18.**

The riches and good things you desire are not far-fetched. They are even closer than ever; obedience is a key to unlock them. Consider **Genesis 22:18** *"And through your descendants, all the nations of the earth will be blessed-all because you have obeyed me."*

> **90.** *"You're in your Now moment, don't be distracted."*
>
> Dr. Laron Matthews, Ph.D.

There is no better time to shine and to get that golden moment you have always desired other than now. Consider **Psalm 102:13** *"Thou shalt arise, and have mercy upon Zion: for the time to favor her, yea, the set time, is come."*

But, if you get distracted, you might lose everything. Stay focused and rid yourself of all distractions. They are all tricks to make you lose out.

> **91.** *"Your voice must become a vaccine against the demonic damage the virus has caused in the earth realms. Prophets are key to the sound in the land. Prophecy pushes you to prophesy."*
>
> Dr. Laron Matthews, Ph.D.

The whole world felt the pain of the pandemic and still do even now. Many people lost loved ones, jobs, businesses, properties, etc. Now is the time you should bring good news and good tidings to the wounded heart.

Allow your voice to serve as an antidote that will fight the demonic destruction released within the earthly realm.

Speaking life and spreading the good news to heal the world should be a priority to you. Your words are more powerful than you think.

Use your words wisely and don't let them break people instead of repairing them. God has made you a prophet and the word of a prophet stands. Consider **Jeremiah 1:5** *"Before I formed thee in the belly I knew thee, and before thou camest forth out of the womb I sanctify thee, and I ordained thee a prophet unto the nations."*

> **92.** *"When you know who you are, don't act like a crisis in the middle of a crisis."*
>
> Dr. Laron Matthews, Ph.D.

Many people lose their footing when things happen out of the ordinary. If you face such a situation, you can allow yourself to panic or fear. It is only the faithless and fearful that lose control when they should take charge. God has not given us the spirit of fear but of strong mind and boldness. Consider **2 Timothy 1:7.**

Your identity gives you the confidence to stand firm and challenge a crisis. Don't shake when you encounter difficulties. When you figure out your place with God, act like it. Consider **2 Corinthians 13:5** *"Examine yourselves, whether ye be in the faith; prove your own selves. Know ye, not your own selves, how that Jesus Christ is in you, except ye be reprobates?"*

> **93.** *"The worst thing you can do is to lie to yourself to please others!"*
>
> Dr. Laron Matthews, Ph.D.

Pleasing others has always been a task no one should accept. Such habit leaves us feeling used, deprived, unsatisfied and hurt. It is good to love yourself first and then love your neighbor as yourself. Don't do things you hate just because you want to make someone else happy. At the end, they won't appreciate it but mock you instead.

People will come into your life and leave, but you will always be with you. You are who you are and people's opinion about you doesn't matter because God's opinion of you stands. Consider **Galatians 1:10** *"For do I now persuade men or God? Or do I seek to please men? For if I yet pleased men, I should not be the servant of Christ."*

> **94.** *"Many people are receiving pathetic words and calling them prophetic words. You must be willing to hear the sound of God over the emotions of the people making your flesh feel good."*
>
> Dr. Laron Matthews, Ph.D.

Many fake prophets are everywhere now. They say things that people want to hear and also make declarations according to how they feel. It's unfortunate that many people believe such words without spiritual backings. Instead of pursuing such empty words, you should be ready to hear the voice of God instead of people's emotional predictions proclaimed to make you feel good.

Hearing directly from God is the best way to decide your life. We are in the end time, and a false prophet will arise. Consider **Matthew 24:24** *"For there shall arise false Christs, and false prophets, and shall shew great signs and wonders; insomuch that, if it were possible, they shall deceive the very elect."*

You must be able to discern the spirit by which people are prophesying into your life. Do not be a victim of false prophecy.

95. *"A true leader must see the world from the eyes of God and not from religious systems or organizations that have been created by men. My heart is not for a building, it's for building God's people for eternal life through His love for them. I truly have a heart for God's people, not a religious agenda that's trying to control the destinies of God's people with their gifts."*

Dr. Laron Matthews, Ph.D.

God has a plan for His people and a true leader should follow that plan. He or she does not have the permission to deviate from the plan of God for His children for the religious system the world works with.

A leader should have a mind of God and think to follow His every command to lead His people. Any leader that deviates is not a true leader. Consider Jeremiah 23:1 *"Woe be unto the pastors that destroy and scatter the sheep of my pasture! Saith the Lord."*

96. *"The number one import of the World is the power of fear,' and the number one export of the World is the presence of death.' The great enemy to both of these is the power of faith.' So faith comes by hearing and by hearing the Word of God."*

Dr. Laron Matthews, Ph.D.

The messages you easily find around you are fear and death. That's what the government will want you to focus on. But to overcome fear and death, you need the authority that comes by "faith." Faith comes by hearing the word of God. Always focus on what God says and not what the government is saying. Don't just believe what they tell you or what they project. Instead, believe and focus on the promises written in the Word of God. Faith takes you higher and makes you untouchable by what rules this world—fear and death.

The one sure place to find faith is in the Word of God. Don't just hear and forget, hear and hear again till it is a part of you. Consider **Romans 10:17** *"So then faith cometh by hearing, and hearing by the word of God."*

> **97.** *"If you have a word from God, you have a ministry. Destiny awaits your sound."*
>
> *Dr. Laron Matthews, Ph.D.*

Once God gives you a word, He expects you to share it and use it to win souls for Him. He will empower you so much that anytime you open your mouth, souls will be won, the sick will be healed, and the captives will be set free. Without that light on you, you'll be wasting your time. So, listen and hear from God.

The world awaits your destiny to shine. So many destinies are waiting for your fulfillment of yours. So, if God sends you a word, then go to the world and resound it to them.

Let people hear you and let them glorify God. Consider **Matthew 5:16** *"Let your light shine before men, that they may see your good works, and glorify your Father which is in heaven."*

> **98.** *"In this season where everything false is becoming real and everything real is becoming false, I, as a prophet of God, must be careful as we release the heart of God to His people. Leaders and people of the Most High God, the ministry is not for magicians, witches, and soothsayers. But, for those who that have a true heart of God and understand the mysteries of the Kingdom of God. So that they can bring His people from the miseries of men's control to the mysteries of the kingdom of God for their destinies and not your games."*
>
> *Dr. Laron Matthews, Ph.D.*

We live in a world of façade, and people misguide people, other people, every day. People are falling into the wrong hands of magicians claiming to be ministers. So, true men of God should double their efforts to bring more people out of the blindfold of witches and magicians in ministry.

True men of God should carefully send the Word of God to His people without mincing words. The times are no longer easy. Consider **2 Timothy 3:1-5** *"This know also, that in the last days perilous times shall come. For men shall be lovers of their own selves, covetous, boasters, proud, blasphemers, disobedient to parents, unthankful, unholy, without natural affection, trucebreakers, false* *accusers, incontinent, fierce, despisers of those that are good, Traitors, heady, highminded, lovers of pleasures more than lovers of God; having a form of Godliness, but denying the power thereof: from such turn away.*

> **99.** *"In whatever you do, don't put your mouth on those that are flawed. One day, they will be 'Free,' according to John 3:16, Isaiah 61:1."*
>
> Dr. Laron Matthews, Ph.D.

When people are going through trying times, do not talk bad about them. Believers who are facing challenges now will be free soon. Consider **John 3:16** *"For God so loved the world, that He gave His only begotten son, that whosoever believeth in Him should not perish, but have everlasting life.*

Instead of speaking badly about them, send good tidings to them. Consider **Isaiah 61:1** *"The Spirit of the Lord God is upon me; because the Lord hath anointed me to preach good tidings unto the meek; He hath sent me to bind up the brokenhearted, to proclaim liberty to the captives, and the opening of the prison to them that are bound;*

> **100.** *"A prophet is a sound that happens within a house; a flawed body that carries the mysteries of the kingdom."*
>
> Dr. Laron Matthews, Ph.D.

A prophet is also human; the difference is the anointing. He is a flawed body that has the mysteries of the kingdom of God.

When a prophet is born into a family, he becomes a voice in the house and his generation.

Consider **Hosea 6:5.**

> **101.** *"You're in the season where the mandate can't be stopped and the purpose can't be aborted, period."*
>
> *Dr. Laron Matthews, Ph.D.*

There is a season for everything, and this is your own time. No matter the plans of the enemy, the purpose of God for your life cannot be terminated.

In these times, no plot can disrupt the mandate of God. God has set out plans for His children and nothing can stop it. Consider **Jeremiah 29:11.**

He has bestowed a purpose for us to fulfill and we will fulfill the purpose. There is nothing anyone can do about it.

> **102.** *"I want to thank God for allowing me to handle eternity in a flawed body so humanity can be delivered and set free."*
>
> *Dr. Laron Matthews, Ph.D.*

God's agenda doesn't depend on your physical health, He's more concerned about your spiritual soundness. God honors His word more than His name and won't stop at anything to bring His word into fulfillment using any vessel that makes himself available.

Moses is a perfect example of a flawed vessel that was used by God to accomplish great works. His stammering tongue didn't hinder him from standing before the Pharaoh of Egypt or leading God's people out of captivity. – **Exodus 4:10-13**.

> **103.** *"God had to take many of us off dependency payroll to put us on faith payroll. Get ready, a sound is getting ready to bless you."*
>
> *Dr. Laron Matthews, Ph.D.*

God, in His infinite mercy, has to remove most of us from depending on others. He then placed us on the path of faith. By trusting in Him, we can have all we need instead of trusting blindly on people who will fail us at any time. So, be prepared to enjoy the blessings of the Lord which are on their way to you.

You can't get supernatural results when you keep sending in natural inputs. You need to start taking your eyes off human connections if you want to experience God's intervention in your situation.

The reason why God has to take some seemingly key personalities out of your life is to make you look back to Him. God didn't take your mom or dad away so that you'll suffer – He wanted you to look up to the ultimate source.

He's the Author and Finisher of our faith – **Hebrews 12:2-3**. This scripture urges us to keep our eyes fixated on Jesus, there's no way He can fail you.

104. *"This is the season to follow the direction of God and not the diversion of man."*

Dr. Laron Matthews, Ph.D.

This is the era in which believers should act by God's directive. It is not the time to allow men to distract you. Many things are happening around us. Fake teachers and prophets are everywhere, teaching false doctrines and selling demonic lies. You must focus entirely on God to protect your soul from devilish deception.

God will direct and instruct you in the right way to go – **Psalm 32:8-9**. It's high time you took your eyes off the world's economy and your meager paycheck. God has something huge in store for you – you only need to take your eyes off man's diversion.

105. *"One of the most challenging human experiences is trying to be you behind a mask that someone else created for you."*

Dr. Laron Matthews, Ph.D.

Human beings are always striving hard to become someone that they are not. They are working so very hard to live a fake life that isn't meant for them. Instead of doing that, be real to yourself and be who God has made you to be. Don't try to follow the part of others and lose yourself in the process. You probably grew up trying to fit into society despite how hard it is to blend in. The truth is that you can never be happy or please God doing that.

Moses grew up in the palace of Pharaoh as an Egyptian prince (Exodus 2:11). This afforded him unimaginable privileges compared to his Hebrew brethren. It takes only a man of purpose to forego all of this, as he did, and choose to share in the plight of fellow Hebrews.

Destiny will always locate you when you pursue God's cause in your place of assignment. Only then can you be who He has called you to be.

> **106.** *"People will give to the vision and purpose of the Kingdom because of the love that God has for them."*
>
> Dr. Laron Matthews, Ph.D.

Due to the love you show to the people around you, they will work towards the Kingdom's purpose and vision. You won't have to force anyone to support God's work. All you need is to be a signpost for the Kingdom and practice what you preach so that your life will be a reflection of the promise ahead.

You can't truly convince any mentally sound person to believe what you believe in without showing them good fruits. You cannot serve God right without faith and faith is a gift of the Holy Spirit.

When you have the Holy Spirit in you, love, which is a fruit of the spirit, will easily radiate through you towards others around you – **Galatians 5:22**. People who feel the love you have for them will naturally want to give to you, innocently projecting the purpose of God through you.

> **107.** *"Before you call people your friend, put them on probation so that they can learn from you as well as you can learn from them. This comes through the manifestation of the God in you and the God in them."*
>
> *Dr. Laron Matthews, Ph.D.*

Sometimes, people keep enemies around them in the name of friends. If you don't check these things, you might be moving about with Judas. So, before making friends with people, set a period of trial for them. That period will help you educate them and also to learn from them.

When you have a cold and a hot object placed in contact with each other, there is no way they'll maintain their initial temperatures. The heat transfer will lower the temperature of one while increasing that of the other.

The same scenario is what happens between friends. There has to be a flow of something, either good or bad. **Proverbs 13:20** admonishes us to be friends with wise people if we want to become wise. Build friendships with fools and you'll suffer calamity.

> **108.** *"Your haters can't take your favor."*
>
> *Dr. Laron Matthews, Ph.D.*

We live in a world where hatred is inevitable whether we deserve it or not – **Psalm 38:9**. Buying a car or a new house can be all it takes to trigger hatred from someone for no just reason.

Be still in God's presence and wait upon him to show up for you **(Psalm 37:7)**. He may delay, but He'll surely intervene. Don't envy sinners or reciprocate hatred to your haters but be careful around them.

> **109.** *"The only thing that the prophets can do is rescue you with the frequency and the Kingdom sound in the earth realms. But God is the only one that can save your soul and give you life."*
>
> *Dr. Laron Matthews, Ph.D.*

God will never do anything on the earth without physical vessels to carry out the required tasks in the earthly realm. Even the devil needs physical vessels. Prophets are God's oracles to discern and proclaim the mind and plans of God for you into existence.

This will give you an easy guide towards fulfilling your God-given destiny. However, it takes a personal relationship with God for your soul to receive salvation. His Holy Spirit will give you the needed guidance to please Him and gain eternal life.

> **110.** *"Don't risk eternal life for external opportunity."*
>
> *Dr. Laron Matthews, Ph.D.*

You'll easily find someone waiting on God when they're in need or trouble. Then, they suddenly stop going to church when they've received answers to their prayers.

Perhaps the only reason why God hasn't given you that job or that brand new house or promotion is that it will threaten your walk with Him. God needs to vet your faith before He can entrust some things into your hands.

God made Esther a queen of Persia during Ahasuerus' reign, not because she was poor or she deserved it. He needed someone in that position because He could see what would come in the future through Haman (**Esther 3-5**).

Your eternity is precious to Him, and He will do everything to keep you from ruining it – you have the ultimate decision, though. God gave you that Job so you can expand His Kingdom on earth using it – which is your primary assignment.

> **111.** *"One of the greatest drawbacks of many people's lives is not knowing their worth in life and their value from life. I approve this destiny statement."*
>
> *Dr. Laron Matthews, Ph.D.*

The greatest stumbling block in people's lives is that they underestimate themselves. They are not aware of their capabilities, usefulness, and what they want from life.

Many people who were destined by God to be great and to fulfill great destinies come to the earth, live, and die without a sense of purpose. This usually happens when you lack a clear revelation of your place in Christ and God's plan for your life.

You are a royal priesthood separated onto God for his purpose and will (**1 Peter 2:9**). You'll never fully enjoy the privileges and benefits available to you if you don't understand what it means to be separated for God.

Spend quality time studying God's potent word for a clearer understanding and revelation of your purpose. Once you understand the greatness you carry inside of you, success will become yours because you'll trust yourself to pursue and achieve great things.

> **112.** *"Great seasons of blessings will know your name, great seasons of opportunity will know your destiny."*
>
> Dr. Laron Matthews, Ph.D.

God doesn't do anything on the surface of the planet without making the choicest portions available to His elect. He says in His word that the plans that He has for you are of good and not of evil, to bring you to an expected end (**Jeremiah 29:11**).

Always stay at the place where He wants you to be; that's where you'll always find whatever blessings He has for you. In your place of purpose, you're bound to encounter opportunities that are highly instrumental in fulfilling your destiny.

> **113.** *"Some of you are feeling lonely right now. Well, you're not (lonely). You're in a place called sacred. God has your gold mine hidden in a Fort Knox 'safe' now, for the right person or people who can afford your combination of the greatness of the value in you."*
>
> Dr. Laron Matthews, Ph.D.

Many of you may feel that you are all alone right now, but you are not. God has hidden your greatness away from the enemy and time wasters to protect your divine value. He is waiting for the right people to bring out the best in you by recognizing these qualities and values divinely bestowed upon you to locate you.

It is quite normal to think that Moses felt lonely when he spent 40 days on Mount Sinai (**Exodus 24:18**). God doesn't need a crowd for Him to work on a man. He wants to have you all to Himself at a place of separation (void of distractions).

Jesus had a good understanding of this. That's why He chose to fast alone in the desert. Another reason why He was separated from His disciples at the Mount of Transfiguration. Be patient with Him while He creates the version of you that will shake the world.

God is Love. Jesus summarized all Ten Commandments into love for God and towards our fellow humans. There's no way you can sin if you have a deep understanding of what it takes to love your neighbor as yourself and God also (**Matthew 22:34-40**).

Love is what will differentiate you as a child of God and make you deal modestly with your fellow humans. Your knowledge of God's abundant love for you is also very important if you must take dominion and gain access to what He has in store for you.

> **114.** *"You must be allergic to stuff that's too cheap for your future."*
>
> Dr. Laron Matthews, Ph.D.

If you value your tomorrow, don't allow things that are worth nothing to destroy it for you. For instance, sin will take you down instead of raising you. So try hard not to allow it to destroy your future. It is the trick of the devil to stop you from reaching the right destination.

The prodigal son left his father's house with all his heritage and squandered it on vanity. This led to a princely son serving pigs and having a share in their leftovers (**Luke 15:11-32**). He was foolish, right?

Almost every one of us has neglected our heritage as sons of God, partaking in things that can be likened to eating swine food. So, you are in no position to judge the prodigal son. Know your place in Christ and avoid anything that will soil that kingly robe he has put on you.

> **115.** *"The custom-made anointing is not costume-made."*
>
> Dr. Laron Matthews, Ph.D.

Everyone has a specific call upon their lives by God (**1 Cor 7:17**). Alongside, God provides them with the necessary anointing needed for the success of their calling. It's their responsibility to discover what their callings are.

What's next is uncovering the preordained path they should follow towards fulfilling that call. Don't limit your anointing to your office as a deacon or chorister in your local church. You have unlimited resources in you; tap from it.

> **116.** *"Our destiny moment should never be connected to a desperate situation because once that moment is released and spoken, desperation will always damage the destiny of that special moment in time. The only impact you have to change someone's life is to protect your destiny in the moment of desperation."*
>
> *Dr. Laron Matthews, Ph.D.*

We all blame Esau for foolishly selling his birthright over some stew (**Genesis 25:29-34**). Esau probably saw his birthright as inconsequential in that dire situation of hunger. Little did he know it would play a major role in shaping his destiny.

Some of us have done worse for something as foolish as an uncontrollable sexual desire. You may not feel the results of your actions until later in the future. Always make sure to consult the Holy Spirit before making decisions; you'll be glad you did.

117. *Don't Forfeit your Destiny and happiness from someone else agenda and madness for your life. Seize your love moment and your priceless time.*

Dr. Laron Matthews, Ph.D.

118. *You know when your future is ready, that's when your past calls or wants you back. Tell them to stop sweating you, you have already showered and dried them off from their mess that was once in your life.*

Dr. Laron Matthews, Ph.D.

119. *When betrayal shows up strength shows out and power prepares you for your next move without "Them"*

Dr. Laron Matthews, Ph.D.

120. *Don't allow being lonely today cheat you out of being scared now for someone's lust story that will leave you broken hearted tonight and empty in the morning.*

Dr. Laron Matthews, Ph.D.

121. *Anyone who cannot see royalty in you cannot be loyal to you and cover the crown from you.*

Dr. Laron Matthews, Ph.D.

122. *Execute the plans of righteousness and the kingdom of darkness will not have power over your purpose and destiny.*

Dr. Laron Matthews, Ph.D.

123. You've been found not guilty in courts of your enemies because love shows up to give passion its victory.

Dr. Laron Matthews, Ph.D.

124. The price of the air must obey the principle when you understand Gods plan for the power within you.

Dr. Laron Matthews, Ph.D.

125. Your unscheduled praise will confuse the devil and stop his words frm shipping.

Dr. Laron Matthews, Ph.D.

PROPHET LARON MATTHEWS.......

Prophet Laron Matthews is known as a seasoned man of God with character, integrity, wisdom, and great revelation of God's Word with Prophetic accuracy. He is a gifted communicator to all facets of people, linking the young and old together to accomplish the vision of Christ (John 17:22) with passion and love for the 21st-century church (Proverbs 17:27). Through this vision, he has crossed denominational barriers to bring the power of fellowship, friendship, and relationship with God's best interest at heart.

"A man that hath friends must shew himself friendly" (**Proverbs 18:24**). Prophet Matthews was born October 31, 1967, the seventh child of 18 children born to Bishop Nathaniel and Mrs. Suzanne Matthews.

Prophet Matthews is a devoted parent and grandfather. He matriculated through Joliet Township High School Central, Joliet Junior College, The Economic Business Institute

Prophet Matthews and was licensed a Minister in February, 1996, he was appointed Chairman of the Finance Committee under the leadership of his father Bishop Nathaniel Matthews of The Way of Life Holiness Church Inc., many other responsibilities came from this gifted area. In July, 1997, he was ordained and appointed

International Youth President of Apostolic Assembly Way of Holiness Church of God Inc., under the Late Bishop George King. He was appointed Financial Accountability person for the Youth Department International and Chairman of the Youth Convention.

Prophet Matthews completed Ministerial Protocol and Etiquette for Leadership, Altar Workers Training, and received Apostolic Prophetic impartation in the ascension Office of Prophet in February 2001 and in September 2006, he was ordained to the office of Pastorate.

Now currently conducting Prophetic explosion crusade meetings and conferences nationally; Prophet Matthews established the inner-city counselors and training program for the Joliet Park District, which re-established and unified one of the greatest inter-governmental agreements in Will County; he was also a member of the Will County Gang Task Force.

Prophet Matthews is presently senior Pastor of Restoration Foundation Prophetic International Ministries, Harvey, IL.

Restoration Destiny Center, San Antonio, Tx

Prophet Laron Matthews is a graduate of American Bible University with a Bachelors Degree in Ministry and a Master's Degree in Christian Counseling Licensed through the New Covenant Christian Counselors Association. Prophet Matthews Also received his Honorary Doctorate Degree From American Bible University in 2017 and his Ph.D. from Global Evangelical Christian College and Seminary of Montgomery, Alabama, in June 2018 in Doctor of Philosophy-Christian Education. Prophet Matthews is the author of a dynamic book "Love The Unfinished Chapter.

In 2021 Dr. Laron Matthews was honored to receive the "PRESIDENTS LIFE TIME ACHIEVEMENT AWARD"

Prophet Laron Matthews is currently the overseer of a dynamic anointed Prophetic Encounter Conference line weekly 5:00 a.m. cst.. You can also join Prophet Matthews On Sunday Mornings 7:00 a.m. cst.

Prophet Matthews had a vision for people to ask questions when they don't feel comfortable asking in their local congregations. If you have a question that you would like to ask and don't feel comfortable asking at your own church? Prophet Laron Matthews invites you to join him and his co-host Evangelist Thelma Sidney every Thursday morning at 5:00 a.m. CST. To call into **"THE THURSDAY MORNING OPEN FORUM."**

218-548-3684 passcode: 435160#.

"Also I heard the voice of the Lord saying, Whom shall I send, and who will go for us? Then said I, Here am I; send me." **Isaiah 6:8**

Contact Prophet Matthews

877-912-2027

708-825-1988

LARONMATTHEWSMINISTRIES@GMAIL.COM

WWW.WERESTOREU.ORG

www.ingramcontent.com/pod-product-compliance
Lightning Source LLC
Chambersburg PA
CBHW071107090426
42737CB00013B/2521